MW01247141

$\mathcal{S}$ir,
more than kisses, letters
mingle souls;
For, thus friends
absent speak.

—JOHN DONNE, verse
from a letter written
to Sir Henry Wotton.

*F*inally
all of *you* *be* of one
mind, having
compassion for one
another, love as brothers,
be tenderhearted, *be*
courteous;

—1 PETER 3:8

*J*udge
not thy friend until thou
standest in his place.

—RABBI HILLEL

*L*et
the soul be assured that
somewhere in the
universe it should rejoin
its friend, and it would
be content and cheerful
alone for a thousand
years.

—EMERSON, *Friendship Essays*

*F*are
thee well, for I
must leave thee,
Do not let this parting
grieve thee,
And remember that the
best of friends must part.

—from the song "There is a
Tavern in the Town,"
ANONYMOUS

*Y*et
in comparison with what
possession, of all others,
he asked, would not a
good friend appear far
more valuable? What
sort of house, or yoke of
oxen, is so useful as a
truly good friend? What
other acquisition is so
beneficial? . . . .

—XENOPHON, from
Memorabilia

Grafted on friendship, it
exalts the mind;
But when the graft no
longer does remain,
The dull stock lives, but
never bears again.

—JOHN DRYDEN, from
Conquest of Granada

*T*hat
friendship which from
withered love
does shoot,
Like the faint herbage
on a rock, wants root;
Love is a tender
amity, refined;

So the bargain was
struck; with the little
god laden,
She joyfully flew to her
home in the grove.
"Farewell," said the
sculptor, "you're not the
first maiden
Who came but for
Friendship, and took
away Love!"

—THOMAS MOORE,
"A Temple to Friendship"

"Oh, never," said she,
"Could I think of
enshrining
An image whose looks
are so joyless and dim;
But yon little god upon
roses reclining,
We'll make, if you
please, sir, a Friendship
of him."

So she flew to the
sculptor, who set down
before her
An image, the fairest his
art could invent;
But so cold, and so dull,
that the youthful adorer
Saw plainly this was
not the Friendship
she meant.

A
Temple to Friendship,"
cried Laura, enchanted,
"I'll build in this garden;
the thought is divine."
So the temple was built,
and she now
only wanted
An image of Friendship,
to place on the shrine.

That teaches me, when
seeming most alone,
Friends are around us,
though no word
be spoken.

—HENRY WADSWORTH
LONGFELLOW, from "As One
Who, Walking in the
Twilight Gloom"

Thanks for the
sympathies that ye
have shown!
Thanks for each kindly
word, each silent token,

And pause, and turn to
listen, as each sends
His words of friendship,
comfort, and assistance.

S_o

walking here in twilight,
O my friends!
I hear your voices,
softened by the distance,

"Deed, and I don't know," said Alan. "For just precisely what I thought I liked about ye, was that ye never quarrelled;—and now I like ye better!"

—ROBERT LOUIS STEVENSON, from *Kidnapped*

$\mathcal{A}$lan,"
cried I, "what makes ye
so good to me? what
makes ye care for such a
thankless fellow?"

My friends are not perfect—no more am I—and so we suit each other admirably. . . .

—ALEXANDER SMITH,
Dreamthorp

*T*he tide of friendship does not rise high on the bank of perfection. Amiable weaknesses and shortcomings are the food of love. . . .

in cases, that keep their
sounds to themselves.
. . . We are born to do
benefits: and what better
or properer can we call
our own than the riches
of our friends? . . .

—SHAKESPEARE,
Timon of Athens

O

you gods, think I, what
need we have any
friends, if we should
ne'er have need of 'em?
they were the most
needless creatures living,
should we ne'er have use
for 'em, and would most
resemble sweet
instruments hung up

*S*he
was in a class by herself.
It is not often that
someone comes along
who is a true friend and
a good writer. Charlotte
was both.

—E. B. WHITE, the last words
from *Charlotte's Web*

*T*here
are three faithful
friends—an old wife,
an old dog,
and ready money.

—BENJAMIN FRANKLIN,
Poor Richard's Almanack

Blush when I tell you
how a bird
A prison with a
friend preferr'd
To liberty without.

—WILLIAM COWPER, from
"The Faithful Bird"

O ye who never taste
the joys
Of Friendship, satisfied
with noise,
Fandango, ball, and rout!

Nor would he quit that
chosen stand
Till I, with slow and
cautious hand,
Return'd him
to his own.

*S*o

settling on his cage,

by play,

And chirp, and kiss,

he seem'd to say,

You must not

live alone—

*N*ature
teaches beasts to know
their friends.

—SHAKESPEARE,
Antony and Cleopatra

*Y*ou
want a friend for life,
get a dog.

—HARRY S. TRUMAN

*A*nimals are such agreeable friends—they ask no questions, they pass no criticisms.

—GEORGE ELIOT,
Scenes of Clerical Life

*M*y

friend must be a bird,

Because it flies!

Mortal my friend

must be,

Because it dies!

Barbs has it, like a bee.

Ah, curious friend,

Thou puzzlest me!

—EMILY DICKINSON,
"My Friend Must be a Bird"

If my friends have
alabaster boxes laid away,
full of fragrant perfumes
of sympathy and
affection, which they
intend to break over my
body, I would rather they
bring them out in my
weary and troubled hours
and open them, that I
may be refreshed and
cheered while I need
them . . .

—GEORGE W. CHILDS,
from *A Creed*

The kind things you
mean to say when they
are gone, say before they
go. The flowers you
mean to send for their
coffin, send to brighten
and sweeten their homes
before they leave them.

Speak approving, cheering words while their ears can hear them, and while their hearts can be thrilled and made happier.

*D*o
not keep the alabaster
box of your love and
tenderness sealed up
until your friends are
dead. Fill their lives
with sweetness.

Better and safer, of
course, are such
friendships, where
disparities of years or
circumstances put the
idea of love out of
the question.

—SIR EDWARD
BULWER-LYTTON

By friendships, I mean pure friendships,—those in which there is no admixture of the passion of love, except in the married state. . . .

A woman, if she be really your friend, will have a sensitive regard for your character, honor, repute. . . .

*I*t

is a wonderful advantage
to a man, in every
pursuit or avocation, to
secure an adviser in a
sensible woman. In
woman there is at once a
subtle delicacy of tact,
and a plain soundness of
judgment, which are
rarely combined to an
equal degree in man.

I praise the Frenchman,
his remark was shrewd,
How sweet, how passing
sweet is solitude!
But grant me still a
friend in my retreat,
Whom I may whisper,
Solitude is sweet.

—WILLIAM COWPER,
"Retirement"

A slender acquaintance with the world must convince every man that actions, not words, are the true criterion of the attachment of friends; and the most liberal professions of good-will are very far from being the surest marks of it.

—GEORGE WASHINGTON

Then let us clasp hands
as we walk together,
And let us speak softly
in low, sweet tone,
For no man knows on
the morrow whether
We two pass on—or but
one alone.

—ELLA WHEELER WILCOX,
from "Growing Old"

But
all true things in the
world seem truer,
And the better things of
earth seem best,
And friends are dearer,
as friends are fewer,
And love is all as our
sun dips west.

but the Deity in me and in them derides and cancels the thick walls of individual character, relation, age, sex, circumstance, at which he usually connives, and now makes many one.

—EMERSON, *Friendship Essays*

*M*y

friends have come to me
unsought. The great God
gave them to me. By
oldest right, by the
divine affinity of virtue
with itself, I find them,
or rather not I,

Running down on the
edge of his garments.
It is like the dew
of Hermon,
Descending upon the
mountains of Zion;
For there the Lord
commanded the
blessing—
Life forevermore.

—PSALM 133

*B*ehold,
how good and how
pleasant, *it is*
For brethren to dwell
together in unity!
It is like the precious oil
upon the head,
Running down
on the beard,
The beard of Aaron,

perhaps he may never experience the necessity of doing so; but we are governed by our imaginations, and they stand there as a solid and impregnable bulwark against all the evils of life.

—REV. SYDNEY SMITH, *Wit and Wisdom of Sydney Smith*

I could not live if I were
alone upon the earth,
and cut off from the
remembrance of my
fellow-creatures. It is not
that a man has occasion
often to fall back upon
the kindness of his
friends;

If I lived under the burning sun of the equator, it would be pleasure for me to think that there were many human beings on the other side of the world who regarded and respected me;

*L*ife
is to be fortified by many
friendships. To love, and
to be loved, is the
greatest happiness.

If we could only realize
this early and arrive at a
liberal view as regards
others in cultivating our
own attitude of mind,
we would be more
conciliatory and try to
collect by the bond of
sentiment what opinion
has dispersed.

—GOETHE

*S*entiments
are what unites people,
opinions what separates
them. Sentiments are a
simple bond that gathers
us together; opinions
represent the principle of
variety that scatters. The
friendships of youth are
founded on the former,
the cliques of old age
are to be blamed
on the latter.

*L*ove
begets love and kindness
begets kindness. This is
the law which knows no
exception. People dislike
us because we have no
more love for them.

—SWAMI RAMDAS

Me too thy nobleness
has taught
To master my despair;
The fountains of my
hidden life
Are through thy
friendship fair.

—EMERSON "Friendship"

All things through thee
take nobler form
And look beyond
the earth,
The mill-round of our
fate appears
A sun-path in thy worth.

My careful heart was free
again—
O friend, my
bosom said,
Through thee alone the
sky is arched,
Through thee the
rose is red,

I fancied he was fled,
And, after many a year,
Glowed unexhausted
kindliness
Like daily sunrise there.

A
ruddy drop of
manly blood
The surging sea
outweighs;
The world uncertain
comes and goes,
The lover rooted stays.

Only
love enables humanity to
grow, because love
engenders life and it is
the only form of energy
that lasts forever.

—MICHEL QUOIST,
With Open Heart

*L*arge
was his bounty, and his
soul sincere,
Heav'n did a recompense
as largely send;
He gave to mis'ry all
he had, a tear,
He gain'd from Heav'n
('twas all he wish'd)
a friend.

—THOMAS GRAY, *Elegy
Written in a Country Churchyard*

*H*e
who is filled with love is
filled with God himself.

—ST. AUGUSTINE OF HIPPO,
On the Trinity

*W*hat
though youth gave
love and roses,
Age still leaves as
friends and wine.

—THOMAS MOORE, from
"Spring and Autumn"

I
count myself in nothing
else so happy
As in a soul
rememb'ring my
good friends.

—SHAKESPEARE,
King Richard the Second

One
friend in a lifetime is
much; two are many;
three are hardly possible.
Friendship needs a
certain parallelism of
life, a community of
thought, a rivalry of aim.

—HENRY BROOKS ADAMS,
The Education of Henry Adams

These add a bouquet
to my wine!
These add a sparkle
to my pine!
If these I tine,
Can books, or fire,
or wine be good?

—ROBERT HINKLEY
MESSINGER, "Old Friends"

*B*ring
Walter good,
With soulful Fred, and
learned Will,
And thee, my alter ego
(dearer still
For every mood).

So rarely found;
Him for my wine,
him for my stud,
Him for my easel,
distich, bud,
In mountain walk!

—ROBERT HINKLEY
MESSINGER, "Old Friends"

Old
Friends to talk!
Ay, bring those
chosen few,
The wise, the courtly
and the true,

I love everything that's old: old friends, old times, old manners, old books, old wine . . . and old friends are best!

—OLIVER GOLDSMITH, from the play *She Stoops to Conquer*

Old
friends and old
wine are best.

—17TH CENTURY PROVERB

Each as he stands
The work of its hands.
Which shall be more
As he was before? . . .
What is its ends
With Friends?

—WILLIAM HENLEY, from
"Friends, Old Friends"

*F*riends

. . . old friends—

So it breaks, so it ends.

There let it rest!

It has fought and won,

And is still the best

That either has done.

*A*fter
the age of forty there
isn't much to live for
except friendship.

—FRANCINE DU
PLESSIX GRAY

*W*e
need old friends to help
us grow old and new
friends to help us
stay young.

—LETTY COTTIN POGREBIN

In body's lust man doth
resemble but base brute;
  True virtue gets and
  keeps a friend, good
  guide of our pursuit.

—NICHOLAS GRIMALD,
     "A Friend"

*O*f
all the heavenly gifts
that mortal men
commend,
What trusty treasure in
the world can
countervail a friend?

*Idem
velle atque edemn nolle, ea
demum firma amicitia est.*

To like and dislike the
same things, that is
indeed true friendship.

—SALLUST, *Catiline*

A friend you have to buy
won't be worth what you
pay for him.

—GEORGE PRENTICE

*W*as
it friend or foe that
spread these lies?
Nay, Who but an infant
questions in such wise?
'Twas one of my most
intimate enemies.

—DANTE GABRIEL
ROSSETTI

A

friend cannot be known
in prosperity: and an
enemy cannot be hidden
in adversity.

—THE APOCRYPHA, *The
Wisdom of Jesus, the Son of Siraeh*

For now we share agreement on sacred things; and you, who formerly led with me a worldly life, have now united with me in the hope of life eternal.

—ST. AUGUSTINE

*H*ow can I put into words the happiness that fills my heart in knowing that he who for a long time was my friend, has now become my true friend?

For our agreement
regarded merely human,
not divine things,
though, of course, there
was mutual benevolence,
and good-will. But now,
things are changed. How
can I express my joy!

—ST. AUGUSTINE

$\mathcal{A}$t
one time my dearest
friend, you had the same
tastes in profane things
as I. But as regards
sacred matters I am
afraid that since I was
not virtuous, our
friendship did not
conform to the more
important part of the
accepted definition.

Such a man is like the shadow of the sundial, which appears in fine weather, and vanishes when there comes a rainy day.

—HORACE SMITH

A
fashionable friend is one
who will dine with you,
game with you, walk or
ride out with you,
borrow money of you . . .

Short
accounts make
long friends.

—BALZAC

With

rue my heart is laden
For golden friends I had,
For many a
rose-lipt maiden
And many a
lightfoot lad.

—ALRED HOUSMAN,
A Shropshire Lad

Parents we can have but
once; and he promises
himself too much, who
enters life with the
expectation of finding
many friends.

—SAMUEL JOHNSON,
Boswell's Life of Johnson

he
longer we live, and the
more we think, the
higher value we learn to
put on the friendship
and tenderness of parents
and of friends.

*F*riends
are thieves of time.

—17TH CENTURY PROVERB

*L*ove
all, trust a few
Do wrong to none; be
able for thine enemy
Rather in power than
use, and keep thy friend
Under thy own life's key;
be check'd for silence,
But never tax'd
for speech.

—SHAKESPEARE, *All's Well that Ends Well*

Just as they are—chaff
and grain together,
knowing that a faithful
hand will take and sift
them, keep what is
worth keeping, and then
with the breath of
kindness, blow the
rest away.

—GEORGE ELIOT

*O*h

the comfort, the
inexpressible comfort of
feeling safe with a
person: having neither
to weigh thoughts nor
measure words, but to
pour them out.

*G*od
send me a friend that
will tell me of my faults.

—18TH CENTURY PROVERB

*H*is
courage foes, his friends
his truth proclaim.

—JOHN DRYDEN,
Absalom and Achitophel

It is only needful to place yourself so that it may come, and then it comes of itself. Ans then everything turns and changes tiself to the best.

—FREDRIKA BREMER

*W*hen
the first time of love is
over, there comes
something better still.
Then comes that other
love; that faithful
friendship which never
changes, and which will
accompany you with its
calm light through the
whole of life.

I know—for when
you came to lend
Me your kind hand, and
call me friend,
God blessed me unaware.

—JAMES RILEY, "Friend of a
Wayward Hour"

$\mathcal{G}$od
bless me?" Why, your
very prayer
Was answered ere you
asked it there,

But thrice the pressure
of your hand—
First
hail—congratulations—
and Your last "God
bless you!" as the train
That brought you
snatched you back again
Into the unknown land.

—JAMES RILEY, "Friend of a
Wayward Hour"

*F*riend
of a wayward hour, you
came
Like some good ghost,
and went the same;
And I within the
haunted place
Sit smiling on your
vanished face,
And talking with—your
name.

No receipt openeth the heart for a true friend; to whom you may impart griefs, joys, fears, hopes, suspicions, counsels, and whatsoever lieth upon the heart to oppress it, in a kind of civil shrift for confession . . .

—FRANCIS BACON,
Of Friendship

The
principal fruit of
friendship is the ease
and discharge of the
fullness and swellings of
the heart, which
passions of all kinds do
cause and induce.

*T*ime,
which strengthens
friendship, weakens love.

—JEAN DE LA BRUYERE,
Les Caracteres

The
laws of friendship are
austere and eternal, of
one web with the laws of
nature and of morals.

—EMERSON, *Friendship Essays*

friends who have definite
hobbies and opinions
about persons and
things, who have their
private beliefs and
respect mine.

—LIN YUTANG,
With Love and Irony

*F*riends
who are spiritually rich
and who can talk dirt
and philosophy with the
same candor,

friends to whom I need
not be polite, and who
will tell me all their
troubles, matrimonial
or otherwise . . .

—LIN YUTANG,
With Love and Irony

want some good friends,
friends who are as
familiar as life itself,

Then dare to be
generous, dauntless
and gay,
Let us merrily pass life's
remainder away;
Upheld by our friends,
we our foes may despise,
For the more we are
envied, the higher
we rise.

—HENRY CAREY, from
"An Honest Friend"

I envy no mortal though
ever so great,
Nor scorn I a wretch for
his lowly estate;
But what I abhore, and
esteem as a curse,
Is poorness of spirit, not
poorness of purse.

What do I want with a friend who judges me? If I welcome a friend to a meal, I ask him to sit down if he limps, and do not ask him to dance.

—ANTOINE DE SAINT EXUPERY, from "Letter to a Hostage"

It is the acceptance of who I am which made you, at need, indulgent to these things. . . I am grateful to you for accepting me as you find me.

There is a need in me to go where I am pure. It is not my formulae nor the things I do that ever enlightened you as to the man I am.

—ANTOINE DE SAINT EXUPERY, from "Letters to a Hostage"

I,
who, like each of us, feel
the need to be
recognized, in you I feel
pure and I go to you.

*W*hen
I ask I am a foe. When I
lend I am a friend.

—16TH CENTURY PROVERB

A real friend is one who walks in when the rest of the world walks out.

—WALTER WINCHELL

Good
will then may be called
the germ of friendship.
. . . It is impossible for
people to be friends who
have felt no good will to
each other . . .

—ARISTOTLE

*B*usiness,
you know, may bring
money, but friendship
hardly ever does.

—JANE AUSTEN, *Emma*

I sought my money
from my friend,
Which I had
wanted long.
I lost my money and
my friend;
Now was that
not a wrong?

—ANONYMOUS

I once had money
and a friend.
Of either, thought
I store.
I lent my money
to my friend,
And took his word
therefore,

The
best way to make or keep
a friend is to *be* a friend.

—ANONYMOUS

*T*wo
are better than one,
because they have a
good reward for
their labor.
For if they fall, one will
lift up his companion.
But woe to him *who is*
alone when he falls, for
he has no one to help
him up.

—ECCLESIASTES 4:9–10

*I*f
you lend a friend five
dollars and never see
him again, it's worth it.

—ANONYMOUS

The
holy passion of
Friendship is of so sweet
and steady and loyal and
enduring a nature that it
will last through a whole
lifetime, if not asked
to lend money.

—MARK TWAIN,
Pudd'nhead Wilson

Will sour his friendships
with regrets;
Giving and getting,
thus alone
A friendship lives—or
dies a-moan.

--ALEXANDER MacLEAN

*H*e
who gets and never gives
Will lose the truest
friend that lives;
He who gives and
never gets

It is friendship. When the heart overflows with gratitude, or with any other sweet and sacred sentiment, what is the word to which it would give utterance? A friend.

—WALTER SAVAGE LANDOR

*I*n
the hour of distress and
misery the eyes of every
mortal turns to
friendship: in the hour
of gladness and
conviviality, what is
your want?

Let me conclude by
saying to you, what I
have had too frequent
occasion to say to my
other remaining old
friends, *the fewer we
become, the more let us
love one another.*

—BENJAMIN FRANKLIN, in a
letter to Mrs. Hewson,
January 27, 1783

*O*ur
friendship has been all
clear sunshine, without
any, the least, clouds in
its hemisphere.

Grant us but that, and grant us courage to endure lesser ills unshaken, and to accept death, loss, and disappointments, as it were straws upon the tide of life.

—ROBERT LOUIS STEVENSON, from *Vailima Papers*

*F*or
our absent loved ones
we implore Thy
loving-kindness. Keep
them in life, keep them
in growing honor; and
for us, grant that we
remain worthy of their
love. For Christ's sake,
let not our beloved blush
for us, nor we for them.

My wealth is the
vision shared,
The sympathy,
The feast of the
soul prepared
By you for me.

—ANNE CAMPBELL, from
Companionship

I
have never been
rich before,
But you have poured
Into my heart's
high door
A golden hoard.

I grow warm thinking of it, and should glow at the thought if all the glaciers of the Alps were heaped over me! Such friends God has given me in this little life of mine!

—CELIA THAXTER

*A*s
you say, we don't need
soft skies to make
friendship a joy to us.
What a heavenly thing
it is; "World without
end," truly.

Who
seeks a friend without a
fault remains without
one.

—TURKISH PROVERB

My only sketch, profile, of Heaven is a large blue sky, and larger than the biggest I have seen in June—and in it are my friends—all of them—every one of them.

—EMILY DICKINSON

marking as it does an
intellectual alienation as
profound, though not as
complete, as that which
separates us from the
dumb animals, is
radically incompatible
with friendship.

—GEORGE SANTAYANA,
from Persons and Places

*T*here
is a gallantry of the
mind which pervades all
conversation with a lady,
as there is a natural
courtesy towards children
and mystics; but such a
habit of respectful
attention,

*N*o
friendship is so cordial or
so delicious as that of
girl for girl; no hatred so
intense and immovable
as that of woman for
woman.

—WALTER SAVAGE LANDOR

*T*here
is in friendship
something of all
relations, and something
above them all. It is the
golden thread that ties
the heart of all
the world.

—JOHN EVELYN

The
endearing elegance of
female friendship.

—SAMUEL JOHNSON,
Rasselas

*F*riends
are true Twins in soul;
They sympathize in
every thing, and have
the same Love and
Aversion.

—WILLIAM PENN,
Fruits of Solitude

It will speak freely, and
act so too; and take
nothing ill where no ill
is meant; nay, where it
is, 'twill easily Forgive,
and forget too,
upon small
Acknowledgements.

—WILLIAM PENN,
Fruits of Solitude

*T*here
can be no Friendship
where there is no
Freedom. Friendship
loves a Free Air, and will
not be penned up in
straight and narrow
Enclosures.

A stone is many years becoming a ruby; take care that you do not destroy it in an instant against another stone.

—SAADI, *Gulistan*

A friend whom you have
been enjoying during
your whole life, you
ought not to be
displeased with
in a moment.

*T*oo
late we learn, a man
must hold his friend
Unjudged, accepted,
trusted to the end.

—JOHN BOYLE O'REILLY,
from "A Lost Friend"

$\mathcal{M}$ake
new friends; but
keep the old,
One is silver and the
other gold.

—BROWNIE GIRL SCOUT
HANDBOOK

a wavering feeler out of
the shell of self; then a
gush of willingness,
giving with both
hands. . .

—SEAN O'FAOLAIN, from
Bird Alone

That
I knew now, who have
for years tried to live
alone, is how people do
meet and join: a first
slight bridge,

because it was friendship
in its first stage when
one is giving all,
spreading out all one's
little riches, not yet
having discovered either
how much it is vain to
offer or expect.

—SEAN O'FAOLAIN, from
Bird Alone

I
felt about us and our talk
an atmosphere quite
new to me.
It was akin to
benevolence and far
more deep and
mysterious than
friendship,

The
bird a nest, the spider a
web, man friendship.

—WILLIAM BLAKE

A friend is the first person
you call with news of
any importance.

—WOODLEIGH HUBBARD,
The Friendship Book

*W*ithout
friends no one would
choose to live, though
he had all other goods.

—ARISTOTLE,
Nicomachean Ethics

$\mathcal{B}$e
thou familiar, but by
no means vulgar;
those friends thou hast,
and their adoption tried,
Grapple them to thy soul
with hoops of steel.

—SHAKESPEARE, *Hamlet*

The
friendship that can cease
has never been real.

—SAINT JEROME, *Letters*

*T*rue
friendship is
never serene.

—MARIE DE
RABUTIN-CHANTAL, the
Marquise de Sevigne, *Lettres
A'Madam De Gringnan*

O! the joys, that came
down shower-like,
Of Friendship, Love,
and Liberty.

—SAMUEL TAYLOR
COLERIDGE, *Youth and Age*

*F*lowers
are lovely; love
is flower-like;
Friendship is a
sheltering tree;

*T*he
crown of these
Is made of love and
friendship, and sits high
Upon the forehead
of humanity.

—JOHN KEATS, *Endymion*

I
was angry with
my friend;
I told my wrath, my
wrath did end.
I was angry with my foe;
I told it not, my wrath
did grow.

—WILLIAM BLAKE,
Songs of Experience

so in a series of
kindnesses there is at
last one which makes
the heart run over.

—JAMES BOSWELL,
Life of Johnson

*W*e
cannot tell the precise
moment when friendship
is formed. As in filling a
vessel drop by drop,
there is at last a drop
which makes it run over;

*T*he
best mirror is
an old friend.

—GEORGE HERBERT,
The Temple

*F*ate
chooses our relatives, we
choose our friends.

—JACQUES DELILLE,
Malheur et Pitie

*T*hink
where man's glory most
begins and ends,
And say my glory
was I had
such friends.

—WILLIAM YEATS, *Last Poems*

*H*ave
no friends not equal
to yourself.

—CONFUCIUS,
The Confucius Analects

*T*rue
happiness
Consists not in the
multitude of friends,
But in the worth
and choice.

--BEN JOHNSON, *Cynthia's
Revels*

*F*or
memory has painted
this perfect day,
With colors that
never fade,
And we find at the end
of a perfect day,
The soul of a friend
we've made.

—CARRIE JACOBS BOND,
from *A Perfect Day*

A

friend should bear his
friend's infirmities,
But Brutus makes mine
greater than they are.

—SHAKESPEARE, *Julius Caesar*

*B*ut
in deed,
A friend is never known
till a man have a need.

—JOHN HEYWOOD, *Proverbs*

Stay"
is a charming word in a
friend's vocabulary.

—A. B. ALCOTT

A

friend is, as it were,
a second self.

—CICERO, *De Amicitia*

Surround
yourself with friendships
for without them you
cannot achieve your
dreams and goals.

—UNKNOWN

It
is a sweet thing,
friendship, a dear balm,
A happy and auspicious
bird of calm,

—SHELLEY, from
"Epipsychidian"

man is an Island, entire
of itself . . .

—JOHN DONNE, *Devotions*

*H*and
grasps at hand, eye lights
eye in good friendship,
And great hearts expand
And grow one in the
sense of this world's life.

—EMERSON

*B*e
slow to fall into
friendship; but when
thou art in continue firm
and constant.

—SOCRATES

*F*riendship,
like the immortality of
the soul, is too good to
be believed.

—EMERSON, *Friendship Essays*

"Where you die, I will die, and there will I be buried. The Lord do so to me, and more also, if *anything but* death parts you and me."

—RUTH 1:16–17

*B*ut
Ruth said, "Entreat me
not to leave you, *or* to
turn back from following
after you; for wherever
you will go, I will go;
and wherever you lodge,
I will lodge; your people
shall be my people, and
your God, my God.

And so the company of
women with men is wont
to happen to the
destruction of virtue.
And yet, this friendship
is not unlawful, but
needful: if it be had with
good soul, and if it be
loved for God, and not
for the sweetness
of the flesh.

—RICHARD ROLLE

*F*riendship betwixt men and women may be perilous, for fair beauty lightly cherishes (easily allures) a frail soul; and temptation soon sets fleshly desire on fire, and ofttimes bring in the sin of the body and soul.

The
most I can do for my
friend is simply to
be his friend.

—THOREAU, *Journal*

*F*riends
have all things
in common.

—PLATO, *Dialogues*

*T*hou
hast great allies;
Thy friends are
exultations, agonies,
And love, and man's
unconquerable mind.

—WILLIAM WORDSWORTH,
To Toussaint L'Ouverture

The wretched have no friends.

—JOHN DRYDEN, *All For Love*

*I*t's
a good thing
To escape death, but it is
not great pleasure
To bring death
to a friend.

—SOPHOCLES, *Oedipus Rex*

*W*e're
tenting tonight on the
old campground,
Give us a song to cheer
Our weary hearts, a song
of home
And Friends we love so
dear.

—WALTER KITTREDGE,
Tenting on the Old Campground

$\mathcal{A}$nd
laughter, learnt of
friends; and gentleness,
In hearts at peace, under
an English heaven.

—RUPERT BROOKE,
The Soldier

*K*eep
your friendships
in repair.

—EMERSON, Uncollected
Lectures: Table Talk

or any trifle of my
bestowing, loved me,
though no show was
made of it; while all the
protestations in the
world would not win my
confidence in one who
set no value on such
little things.

—WASHINGTON IRVING

*T*here
is after all something in
those trifles that friends
bestow upon each other
which is an unfailing
indication of the place
the giver holds in
the affections. I would
believe that one who
preserved a lock of hair,
a simple flower,

As benefits forgot:
Though thou the
waters warp,
Thy sting is not so sharp
As friend
remembered not.

—SHAKESPEARE,
As You Like It

*M*ost
friendship is feigning,
most loving mere folly:
Then heigh-ho,
the holly!
This life is most jolly.
Freeze, freeze, thou
bitter sky,
That dost not bite
so nigh . . .

*S*o
long as we love we serve;
so long as we are loved
by others, I might say
that we are
indispensable; and no
man is useless while he
has a friend.

—ROBERT LOUIS
STEVENSON, *Across the Plains*

*F*riendship
should not be all
on one side.

—17TH CENTURY PROVERB

*E*very
one that flatters thee
Is no friend in misery.
Words are easy, like
the wind;
Faithful friends are
hard to find.

—RICHARD BARNFIELD,
Poems: In Diverse Humours

$\mathcal{B}$etter
be a nettle in the side of
your friend than
his echo.

—EMERSON, *Friendship Essays*

This
act of kindness did me
an unspeakable amount
of good; for it came
when I most needed to
be assured that anybody
thought it worthwhile to
keep me from sinking."

—NATHANIEL HAWTHORNE

find a true friend, you
must be one.

A true friend loves.

A
true friend you
can count on.

A
true friend will still be a
friend even when
you're not.

A true friend is there when
you need and ask.

*D*ifficult
as it is really to listen to
someone in affliction, it
is just as difficult for him
to know that compassion
is listening to him.

—SIMONE WEIL,
Waiting on God

*T*rue
friendship is a plant of
slow growth, and must
undergo and withstand
the shocks of adversity
before it is entitled to
the appellation.

—GEORGE WASHINGTON,
letter to Bushrod Washington,
January 15, 1783.

*I*ntimacy
creates the best of
human connections—a
soul relationship.

—ANONYMOUS

Friend:
a supporter or
sympathizer (a friend
of labor).

—WEBSTER'S NEW WORLD
DICTIONARY

*F*ame
is the scentless
sunflower, with gaudy
crown of gold;
But friendship is the
breathing rose, with
sweets in every fold.

—OLIVER WENDELL
HOLMES, SR., "No Time Like
the Old Time"

*P*rosperity
makes friends, adversity
tries them.

—PUBLILIUS SYRUS, *Maxim*

And loved so well a
high behavior
In man or maid that
thou from speech
refrained,
Nobility more nobly
to repay?—
O be my friend, and
teach me to be thine!

—EMERSON, "Forbearance"

*H*ast
thou named all the birds
without a gun;
Loved the wood-rose,
and left it on its stalk;
At rich men's tables
eaten bread and pulse;
Unarmed, faced danger
with a heart of trust;

$\mathscr{F}$riend:

A person on the same
side in a struggle.

—WEBSTER'S NEW WORLD
DICTIONARY

*F*riendships
exist everywhere—where
people are struggling
with the trials, and
savoring the joys of life.

—ANONYMOUS

*M*isfortune
shows those who are not
really friends.

—ARISTOTLE, *Endemian Ethics*

he
reason why we allow our
closest friendships to be
broken up is because we
cannot be content with
simply having the other
person, we want the
other person's feelings
as well.

—HUBERT VAN ZELLER,
We Work While the Light Lasts

*O*ur
life's dreams, aspirations,
tributes, successes,
challenges, and defeats
are perceived through
the hearts of our friends.

—ANONYMOUS

The
main legacy we leave
behind when we die are
friends and their
memories of our lives.

—ANONYMOUS

A sprig of
encouragement
A ton of support
A bit of confidence
A bunch of commitment
And a whole lot of fun

—ANONYMOUS

RECIPE FOR A FRIEND

A teaspoon of respect

A tablespoon of trust

A cup of love

A pinch of tolerance

A clove of understanding

$\mathcal{B}e$ a friend to thyself and others will befriend thee.

—18TH CENTURY PROVERB

*H*ave
but few friends though
many acquaintances.

—17TH CENTURY PROVERB

From
acquaintances, we
conceal our real selves.
To our friends we reveal
our weaknesses.

—CARDINAL BASIL HUME,
Searching for God

The
highest privilege there
is, is the privilege of
being allowed to share
another's pain. You talk
about your pleasures to
your acquaintances; you
talk about your troubles
to your friends.

—FR. ANDREW SDC,
Seven Words from the Cross

than a friend to whom
we may turn for
consolation in time of
trouble—and with whom
we may share our
happiness in time of joy.

—ST. AELRED OF RIEVAULX,
Christian Friendship

*N*o
medicine is more
valuable, none more
efficacious, none better
suited to the cure of all
our temporal ills

Be courteous to all, but intimate with few; and let those few be well tried before you give them your confidence.

—GEORGE WASHINGTON,
letter to Bushrod Washington,
January 15, 1783

*W*hen
a friend laughs, it is for
him to disclose the
subject of his joy; when
he weeps, it is for me to
discover the cause
of his sorrow.

—JOSEPH FRANCOIS
DESMAHIS, *Sorrow*

Jesus knows our every
weakness, . . .
In His arms He'll take
and shield thee,
Thou wilt find a solace
there.

—JOE SCRIVEN, words from
hymn "What a Friend We Have
in Jesus"

What
a friend we have
in Jesus, . . .
Can we find a friend
so faithful
Who will all our
sorrows share?

A
man *who has* friends
must himself be friendly
(or may come to ruin),
But there *is* a friend *who*
. sticks closer than
a brother.

—PROVERBS 18:24

*H*owever,
Jesus did not permit
him, but said to him,
"Go home to your
friends, and tell them
what great things the
Lord has done for you,
and how He has had
compassion on you."

—MARK 5:19

Then why should I sit in
   the scorner's seat
Or hurl the cynic's ban?
Let me live in my house
   by the side of the road
And be a friend to man.

—SAM WALTER FOSS,
from "The House by the Side of
the Road"

*L*et
me live in my house by
the side of the road
Where the race of men
go by—
They are good, they are
bad, they are weak,
they are strong,
Wise, foolish,—so am I.

*T*rue
friendship's laws are by
this rule express'd,
"Welcome the coming,
speed the parting guest."

—ALEXANDER POPE,
The Translation of the Odyssey

*D*on't
walk in front of me
I may not follow
Don't walk behind me
I may not lead
Walk beside me
And just be my friend.

—ALBERT CAMUS

Then Jonathan said to David, "go in peace since we have both sworn in the name of the Lord, saying, 'May the Lord be between you and me, and between your descendants and my descendants, forever.'" So he arose and departed, and Jonathan went into the city.

—1 SAMUEL 20:41–42

*N*ow
as soon as the lad had
gone, David arose from a
place toward the south,
fell on his face to the
ground, and bowed down
three times. And they
kissed one another, and
then wept together, but
David more so.

*F*riendship
as the union of two
selves lies beyond
happiness or
unhappiness. It is simply
the other side of our life
and thus free from
all danger.

—LADISLAUS BOROS,
Hidden God

*F*rom
quiet homes and
first beginning,
Out to the undiscovered
ends,
There's nothing worth
the fear of winning,
But laughter and the
love of friends.

—HILAIRE BELLOC, from
Dedicatory Ode

*T*rue
friendship requires
vulnerability

—ANONYMOUS

*T*he
quickest way to lose a
friend is to have
expectations.
The quickest way to gain
a friend is to have
acceptance.

—ANONYMOUS

The sad account of
fore-bemoaned moan.
Which I new pay as if
not paid before.
But if the while I think
on thee, dear friend,
All losses are restor'd
and sorrows end.

—SHAKESPEARE, *Sonnet
XXXb*

I'd
woe,
And moan th' expense
of many a vanish'd sight.
Then can I grieve at
grievances foregone,
And heavily from woe to
woe tell o'er

Then can I drown an
eye (unus'd to flow)
For precious friends hid
in death's dateless night,
And weep afresh love's
long since cancel.

—SHAKESPEARE, *Sonnet
XXXa*

*W*hen
to the sessions of sweet
silent thought
I summon up
remembrance of
things past,
I sigh the lack of many
a thing I sought
And with old woes new
wail my dear
time's waste.

Wherever
you are, it is your own
friends who make
your world.

—RALPH BARTON PERRY,
*The Thought and Character of
William James*

*E*ver

been the best of friends!

—CHARLES DICKENS,
Great Expectations

*M*ake
yourself necessary
to someone.

—EMERSON

If
you would be loved, love
and be loveable.

—BENJAMIN FRANKLIN,
Poor Richard's Almanack

friend in need is
a friend indeed.

—LATIN PROVERB

*I*f
a man does not make
new acquaintances as he
advances through life, he
will soon find himself
left alone. A man,
Sir, should keep
his friendship in
constant repair.

—SAMUEL JOHNSON,
James Boswell's Life of Johnson

*H*e
who has a thousand
friends had not a
friend to spare,
And he who has one
enemy will meet him
everywhere.

—ALI IBN-ABI-TALIB,
"A Hundred Sayings"

I
breathed a song
into the air,
It fell to earth, I knew
not where. . . .
And the song, from
beginning to end,
I found again in the
heart of a friend.

—HENRY WADSWORTH
LONGFELLOW, "The Arrow
and the Song"

"Greater love has no one
than this, than to lay
down one's life
for his friends.
"You are My friends if
you do whatever I
command you."

—JOHN 15:12–14

*T*his
is My commandment,
that you love one
another as I have
loved you.

*Y*ou
and I ought not to die
before we have explained
ourselves to each other.

—JOHN ADAMS, in a letter to
Thomas Jefferson, July 15, 1813

The
only reward of virtue is
virtue; the only way to
have a friend is
to be one.

—EMERSON, *Friendship Essays*

*S*hare
something of yourself so
it is a give/take and
win/win relationship.
Be yourself, who you
really are on the inside.
Realize that you need
that person in your
life and treat them
that way—priorities
will follow.

—ANONYMOUS

*A*ccept
your friend for who
they are.
Don't be afraid to look
them in the eye and tell
them the hard truth.
Support them in their
dreams and endeavors.
Empathize with them,
but don't wallow in their
self-pity and worries.

—ANONYMOUS

I
find friendship to be like
wine, raw when new,
ripened with age, the
true old man's milk and
restorative cordial.

—THOMAN JEFFERSON, in a
letter to Benjamin Rush,
August 17, 1811

He who receives an idea from me, receives instruction himself without lessening mine; as he who lights his taper at mine, receives light without darkening me.

—THOMAS JEFFERSON

Love's fires glow
the longest,
Yet a wrong is
always wrongest,
In Kentucky.

—JAMES MULLIGAN,
In Kentucky

*T*he
moonlight is the softest,
in Kentucky,
Summer days come
oftest, in Kentucky,
Friendship is
the strongest,

A friend is a person with
whom I may be sincere.
Before him I may
think aloud.

—EMERSON, *Friendship Essays*

*W*ords,
once my stock, are
wanting to commend So
great a poet and so
good a friend.

—JOHN DRYDEN, *To My
Friend Mr. Mottex*

I don't know how that is. God is not so wary as we, else He would give us no friends, lest we forget Him.

—EMILY DICKINSON

$\mathcal{M}$y

friends are my estate.
Forgive me then the
avarice to hoard them.
They tell me those who
were poor early have
different views of gold.

To have loved, to have
thought, to have done;
To have advanced true
friends, and beat down
baffling foes?

—MATTHEW ARNOLD,
Empedocles on Etna

Is

it so small a thing
To have enjoyed the sun,
To have lived light in
the spring,

Or help one
fainting robin
Unto his nest again
I shall not live in vain.

—EMILY DICKINSON from "If
I Can Stop One Heart
From Breaking"

I
f

I can stop one heart
from breaking,
I shall not live in vain;
If I can ease one life
the aching,
Or cool one pain,

as monuments of other
men are overgrown with
moss; for our friends
have no place in
the graveyard. ·

—THOREAU, *A Week on the
Concord and Merrimak Rivers*

*E*ven
the death of friends will
inspire us as much as
their lives. . . Their
memories will be
encrusted over with
sublime and pleasing
thoughts,

I

die adoring God, loving
my friends, not hating
my enemies, and
detesting superstition.

—VOLTAIRE

*L*ife
without friends; death
without a witness.

—GEORGE HERBERT

I had three chairs in my
house: one for solitude,
two for friendship,
three for society.

—THOREAU, *Walden*

*H*appy
is the house that
shelters a friend.

—EMERSON, *Friendship Essays*

A
true friend unbosoms
freely, advises justly,
assists readily, adventures
boldly, takes all patiently,
defends courageously,
and continues a friend
unchangeably.

—WILLIAM PENN, *Some Fruits
of Solitude*

*T*here
are three classes of
friendship and enmity,
since men are so
disposed to one another
either by preference or
by need or through
pleasure and pain.

—PTOLEMY, *Tetrabiblos*

A woman once commented, "The best thing a friend ever told me while I was in depression was, 'You know we're getting pretty tired of this. When are you going to do something about it?' That's all it took. I went for help right away."

—ANONYMOUS

I
had many things to
write, but I do not wish
to write to you with
pen and ink;
but I hope to see you
shortly, and we shall
speak face to face. Peace
to you. Our friends greet
you. Greet the friends
by name.

—3 JOHN 13–14

*W*hat
is a friend? A single soul
in two bodies.

—ARISTOTLE

A friend may well be the masterpiece of Nature.

—EMERSON, *Friendship Essays*

*F*riends
are born, not made.

—HENRY BROOKS ADAMS,
The Education of Henry Adams

If
we love one another,
nothing, in truth, can
harm us, whatever
mischances may happen.

—HENRY WADSWORTH
LONGFELLOW

To one idea fondly
clings;
Friendship! that thought
is all thine own,
Worth worlds of bliss,
that thought alone—
"Friendship is Love
without his wings!"

—LORD BYRON, *"Friendship is
Love Without His Wings"*

*T*hrough
few, but chequer'd years,
What moments have
been mine!
Now half obscured by
clouds of tears,
Now bright in rays
divine;
Howe'er my future doom
be cast,
My soul, enraptured with
the past,

One firm record, one
lasting truth
Celestial consolation
brings;
Bear it, ye breezes,
to the seat
Where first my heart
responsive beat—
"Friendship is Love
without his wings!"

—LORD BYRON, *"Friendship is
Love Without His Wings"*

*W*hy
should my anxious
breast repine,
Because my youth
is fled?
Days of delight may still
be mine;
Affection is not dead.
In tracing back the
years of youth,

Friendship
is a word the very sight
of which in print makes
the heart warm.

—AUGUSTINE BIRRELL

Published in Nashville, Tennessee, by Thomas Nelson, Inc., Publishers, and distributed in Canada by Word Communications, Ltd., Richmond, British Columbia, and in the United Kingdom by Word (UK), Ltd., Milton Keynes, England.

ISBN: 0-7852-8162-2

Printed in Hong Kong.
1 2 3 4 5 6 — 97 96 95 94

Forever
F R I E N D S

Thomas Nelson Publishers
NASHVILLE